REPTILES

by
Steffi Cavell-Clarke

©2019
The Secret Book
Company
King's Lynn
Norfolk PE30 4LS

ISBN: 978-1-78998-026-4

A catalogue record for this book
is available from the British Library.

Written by:
Steffi Cavell-Clarke

Edited by:
Charlie Ogden

Designed by:
Drue Rintoul

Photocredits
Abbreviations: l–left, r–right, b–bottom, t–top, c–centre, m–middle.

Front Cover – Anest, Narupon Nimpaiboon, pets in frames, Chansom Pantip, PetlinDmitry. 4l – Marques. 4b – Philip Evans. 5 – Rich Carey. 6 – Christopher Mansfield. 7tl – Business stock. 7tr – Brandon Alms. 8tl – Eric Isselee. 8bl – Andrew Burgess. 8tr – Eric Isselee. 8br – Rudmer Zwerver. 9 – Mark52. 10 – Eric Isselee. 11 – alexilena. 12ml – Aleksey Stemmer. 12br – Lana Langlois. 12bl – Tungphoto. 13 – tropicdreams. 14 – Kuttelvaserova Stuchelova. 15t – underworld. 15b – Michiel de Wit. 16bl – Vladimir Wrangel. 16br – okanakdeniz. 17 – nattanan726. 18 – Cathy Keifer. 19 – EpicStockMedia. 20t – Matt Jeppson. 20b – ANDRZEJ GRZEGORCZYK. 21 – cellistka. 22t – Heiko Kiera. 22b – Paul Tessier. 23t – Joyce Mar. 23b – Heiko Kiera. 24 – cellistka. 25 – Lidiya Oleandra. 26 – Eric Isselee. 27 – Ryan M. Bolton. 28 – KRISS75. 29 – Fotos593. Images are courtesy of Shutterstock.com, unless stated otherwise. With thanks to Getty Images, Thinkstock Photo and iStockphoto.

All facts, statistics, web addresses and URLs in this book were verified as valid and accurate at time of writing. No responsibility for any changes to external websites or references can be accepted by either the author or publisher.

CONTENTS

Words that look like <u>this</u> are explained in the glossary on page 31.

THE ANIMAL KINGDOM

The animal kingdom includes over 1 million known living <u>species</u>. They come in many different shapes and sizes, they each do weird and wonderful things and they live all over planet Earth.

From the freezing Arctic waters to the hottest desert in the world, animals have <u>adapted</u> to often extreme and diverse conditions on Earth.

Even though each and every species of animal is <u>unique</u>, they still share certain characteristics with each other. These shared characteristics are used to classify animals. There are six main groups used to classify animals. They are: mammals, reptiles, birds, insects, amphibians and fish.

Around **10,000 new** species of animal are discovered **every year.**

Reptiles include turtles, lizards, snakes and crocodiles.

REPTILES

WHAT IS A REPTILE?

Reptiles have backbones and their skin is almost completely covered in scales. Most reptiles lay soft-shelled eggs on land.

Reptiles usually live on land, but some, such as turtles and crocodiles, can also live in water. Reptiles are cold-blooded animals, which means that their body temperatures change depending on the temperature of their environments.

Great Lakes bush vipers can be found near water in Africa.

There are around 10,000 different species of reptile in the world today. Many species look different from one another and have their own individual features that help them to survive in their habitats. Snakes, lizards, crocodiles and tortoises are all types of reptile.

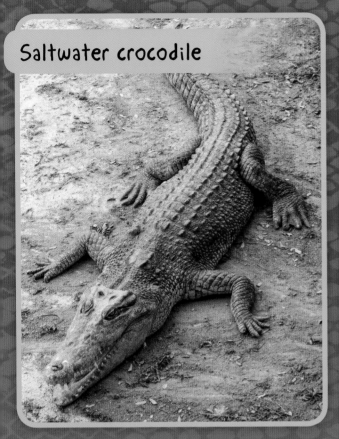

Saltwater crocodile

Leaf chameleon

The largest reptile on Earth is the saltwater crocodile, which can grow up to six metres (m) long, whilst the leaf chameleon is the smallest reptile on Earth measuring in at around three centimetres (cm) long.

REPTILE CHECKLIST

- Usually lay eggs
- Breathe using lungs
- Skin covered in scales
- Cold-blooded
- <u>Vertebrate</u>

BODY PARTS

Even though all species of reptile are unique, they can still be grouped together by their shared characteristics. Each class of animal can be broken down into smaller groups called orders. Animals i same order are even more simi one another than those in the class. The reptile class has fou main orders.

TORTOISES AND TURTLES

Tortoises and turtles have bony shells on their backs that are covered in horny plates called scutes. Many species hide in their shells when they sense danger.

SNAKES AND LIZARD

Snakes are reptiles that hav long, flexible bodies and n legs. Lizards have four <u>limb</u> and a tail. Some lizards hav long tongues that they use to catch <u>prey</u>.

CROCODILES AND ALLIGATORS

Crocodiles and alligators are large reptiles with powerful jaws and tails. They spend most of their time in water.

TUATARAS

Tuataras have spiky scale called spines, down the cer of their backs and look ve similar to lizards.

SHELLS

Tortoises and turtles are the only vertebrates that have bony shells. This unique characteristic offers them protection from <u>predators</u> in a number of ways. Many species can tuck their heads and legs inside their shells to protect their soft body parts. However, there are a few species that cannot hide in their shells, such as sea turtles. All tortoises and turtles have dome-shaped shells that make it particularly difficult for predators to crush them in their jaws.

Dome-shaped shell

Shells can also help to <u>camouflage</u> turtles and tortoises as their dark-green colours allow them to blend in with their surroundings.

SCALES

A reptile's skin is covered in scales that help to protect its body. Scales also help to keep water inside of the reptile's body, which means that many species of reptile are good at surviving in hot, dry desert habitats. The scales also act like a suit of armour that protects the animal from dirt and harmful parasites. A reptile's scales can break and so many reptiles are able to shed their skin and grow new scales to replace the ones they have lost.

Scales are made of keratin, which is the same material that fingernails are made out of.

COLD-BLOODED

Reptiles are cold-blooded animals, which means that their body temperatures change with the temperature of their environments. To give themselves <u>energy</u>, they warm their bodies up using the heat of the Sun. Once warm, they will have the energy to be able to move around and find food and shelter.

Being cold-blooded means that reptiles can't keep themselves warm if their environment is cold. Because of this, cold climates can be very dangerous for reptiles, which is why most reptiles live in warmer parts of the world.

When a reptile sunbathes, it is called **basking**.

GETTING AROUND

Reptiles move in many different ways. Most reptiles get around by walking or running on four legs but other reptiles can also swim, jump and slither!

Tortoises have four legs that carry their bodies and shells.

Sea turtles have large flippers that help them to push through the water.

Snakes slither across the ground by moving the muscles in their bodies. They are able to climb trees and rocks by gripping onto them with the large scales on their stomachs.

Lizards use four legs to walk, run and jump. They usually use their tails for balance and to grip onto things, such as the branches of trees.

Crocodiles and alligators have four short legs that they use to walk and swim.

BREATHING

All reptiles breathe using <u>organs</u> called lungs. The lungs pull in and push out air with the help of a muscle called the diaphragm, which sits just under the ribcage. <u>Oxygen</u> in the air enters the body through the mouth and nose, fills the lungs and passes into the <u>bloodstream</u>. Reptiles, like all other animals, need oxygen in order to survive.

Sea turtles are <u>aquatic</u> reptiles. This means that they have adapted to live mostly in water instead of on land. Turtles can hold their breath for between four and seven hours while underwater.

Read more about turtle adaptations on **page 19!**

Sea turtle

PREDATORS AND PREY

All animals can be sorted into groups depending on what they eat. The three groups are carnivores, herbivores and omnivores.

Herbivores
Plant-eaters

Carnivores
Meat-eaters

Omnivores
Plant- and meat-eaters

Most reptiles are carnivores, eating animals such as rodents and insects. Other reptiles, such as tortoises, are herbivores and only eat plants and fruit. There are also omnivorous reptiles, such as the box turtle, that eat things such as fish, frogs, flowers and berries.

14

Animals that hunt other animals are called predators, while animals that are hunted by other animals are called prey. Crocodiles are predatory carnivores. They hunt their prey by swimming along with just their eyes and ears above the water's surface.

They wait for their prey to come within reach and then they launch towards them. They grip their prey between their strong, sharp teeth.

Crocodiles have powerful muscles that clamp their jaws together. The saltwater crocodile has the **strongest** bite of any animal.

DESERTS, RAINFORESTS AND SWAMPS

Habitats provide food and shelter for the animals and plants that live in them. Most reptiles live in warm habitats such as deserts and dry <u>grasslands</u>. It may seem that hardly any life can survive in the desert, but some animals and plants have learnt how to survive in these extreme environments. Reptiles need very little food or water, which helps them to survive in places where these things are hard to find, such as the desert. Instead, they mostly use the Sun's heat to give them the energy they need in order to move. Tropical rainforests are home to a huge variety of reptiles. The Amazon rainforest is the world's largest tropical rainforest. It provides a wide range of habitats for the animals that live there, such as caves, swamps and tall trees.

Deserts make up around **25 percent** of all the land on Earth.

The Amazon rainforest is home to **one-tenth** of the known species on Earth.

Alligators and crocodiles often live near to swamps where there is a lot of mud and water. They are mostly found in <u>tropical regions</u> of the world, such as Africa and Central America. Water helps alligators and crocodiles to blend in with their environment, making it easier for them to take their prey by surprise. Crocodiles and alligators hunt many different types of prey. This means that they are more likely to survive as they have a wider range of prey to choose from than some other animals.

ADAPTATION

Reptiles have lived on Earth for over 300 million years. Over time, they have adapted to suit their environments in many amazing ways.

Chameleons are known for being able to change colour. They do this to help control their body temperature. When they are cold, they become darker, and when they are hot, they become lighter. A change in colour can also be used to work out how chameleons are feeling – brighter colours often mean they are excited!

Leaf-tail lizard

Many other lizards use camouflage in order to disguise themselves. The colour of the leaf-tail lizard's skin allows it to perfectly blend in with trees and leaves.

Unlike most other reptiles, turtles spend much of their lives in water and their bodies have adapted to be able to survive in these habitats. Turtles have lungs, which means that they have to come up to the water's surface in order to breathe. However, they can swim underwater for hours at a time without coming up for air. They are able to store lots of oxygen in their blood and muscles. When they move their flippers, they pump oxygen into their lungs, which allows them to continue swimming without having to breathe through their mouths.

LIFE CYCLES

A life cycle is the series of changes that a living thing goes through from the start to the end of its life. Usually, reptiles start life inside soft-shelled eggs, which they eventually hatch out of. However, not all reptiles lay eggs – some species give bir[t] to live young that develop inside the female. Most reptiles do not look after their eggs. Instead, the[y] bury them in the ground and lea[ve] them to hatch on their own.

Even sea turtles return to land in order to lay their eggs.

Unlike other reptiles, female crocodiles and alligators look after their young. Crocodiles bury their eggs in nests by rivers and wait nearby for around three months until their eggs hatch. During this time, the mother crocodile will protect her eggs from predators and other dangers. When the baby crocodiles hatch, they start to make a chirping noise. Their mother will dig down to the nest before carefully carrying her babies to the water's edge in her mouth. A mother crocodile will stay with her babies for a few weeks until they have grown larger and can survive on their own.

A mother crocodile can carry up to 15 babies in her mouth at one time.

A Burmese python is a large snake that lives in tropical rainforests in Asia. A mother python carries her eggs inside herself for roughly three months before laying them. Burmese pythons can lay up to 100 eggs at a time and they stay with their eggs for six to eight weeks. Mothers keep their eggs warm by vibrating their muscles until the eggs are ready to hatch. Once the eggs hatch, their mother will leave and the baby pythons must survive on their own.

A Burmese python can grow to over five metres long. At the age of four or five, the snake will be ready to <u>mate</u> and produce more baby pythons.

As the young Burmese pythons – called snakelets – grow, their scaly skin will stretch. Unlike human skin, a snake's skin reaches a point where it cannot grow any bigger. When this occurs, a new layer of skin grows underneath and as soon as it is complete, the old skin peels away. Most snakes shed their skin between two and four times every year.

An adult Burmese python will make its home in a cave or tree and will hunt other animals for food. Burmese pythons are constrictors, meaning that they use their strong muscles to squeeze their prey to death. They do this by biting their prey, wrapping their long bodies around them and then squeezing.

EXTREME REPTILES

Some reptiles have developed extreme habits or skills that help them to survive.

GIANT ANACONDA

An anaconda has a long, thick body with strong, powerful muscles. It has a thick, scaly skin that is dark green, yellow and black, which helps it to blend in with trees and the ground. Anacondas often lie in shallow swamps and streams, waiting for their prey to pass.

The anaconda is a constrictor, meaning that it wraps itself around its prey and squeezes it until it dies. A record-breaking anaconda measured in at 8.43 metres (m) from head to tail. That's longer than a bus!

Anacondas don't lay eggs. They give birth to up to 80 **live** snakes at one time.

Size:
4.6 m long

Home:
Rainforests in
South America

Diet:
Fish, birds
and mammals

GALÁPAGOS GIANT TORTOISE

The Galápagos tortoise is the largest living species of tortoise on the planet. They are only found on the Galápagos Islands in the Pacific Ocean. They are extremely peaceful creatures and like to spend their days grazing on grass and leaves, as well as basking in the sun. They sleep for nearly 16 hours every day! Their huge bodies can store large amounts of water, which means that they can survive for up to a year without eating or drinking.

The oldest Galápagos tortoise that ever lived reached **175 years old!**

Size:
1.5 m long

Home:
Galápagos Islands

Diet:
Plants and fruit

KOMODO DRAGON

The Komodo dragon is a huge reptile that lives on Indonesian islands. Komodo dragons are the world's heaviest lizards and they are deadly predators. They will eat almost anything they find, including deer, fish and even humans! When a Komodo spots its prey, it springs into action and uses its sharp claws to hold the animal down. A quick bite with its sharp teeth allows the Komodo to pass <u>venom</u> into its prey. The Komodo dragon does this because if the prey escapes, the venom will weaken it and the Komodo dragon will still be able to finish its meal.

Size:
3 m long

Home:
Grasslands on Indonesian islands

Diet:
Large and small animals and even humans

ALLIGATOR SNAPPING TURTLE

The alligator snapping turtle is one of the largest freshwater turtles in the world. It has a spiky shell, beak-like jaws and a thick, scaly tail. The alligator snapping turtle spends most of its time lurking in murky waters in swamps and shallow, freshwater rivers. This turtle has one of the most unique hunting methods of all reptiles. On the end of its tongue is a small, pink piece of skin that looks like a worm. The turtle wiggles this worm-like piece of skin in order to attract prey. Fish, frogs and birds can all mistake this for a juicy, wriggling worm and then jump straight into the turtle's mouth.

Size:
80 cm long

Home:
Southeastern United States

Diet:
Small animals and aquatic plants

REPTILES UNDER THREAT

HABITAT DESTRUCTION

According to some scientists, almost one-fifth of the world's reptile species are at risk of <u>extinction</u>. One of the biggest threats towards reptiles is the disruption or destruction of their natural habitats. As the human population grows, towns and cities are built in areas of land that are important habitats for reptiles and other animals. Large areas of forest around the world have been burnt down or cleared for farmland or housing. This has left many animals unable to find shelter and food, leaving them unable to survive.

WATER POLLUTION

Human waste and <u>pollution</u> has affected animal life around the world – from the thickest jungle to the deepest ocean. The rubbish in the world's oceans comes from many places, including rubbish that is thrown into rivers and then flows into the sea. Once in the ocean, the rubbish can last for years, creating great danger for the animal life in the area. Sea turtles all over the world often get caught in rubbish that is in the oceans and many of these eventually die. It is extremely important that we never throw rubbish on the ground or into water so that we do not end up putting animals in danger.

FIND OUT MORE

BOOKS

Reptiles (Living Things & Their Habitats) by Grace Jones

(BookLife, 2017)

Animal Classification (Discover & Learn) by Steffi Cavell-Clarke

(BookLife, 2017)

WEBSITES

WWF

www.wwf.org.uk

On this website you can follow links to information on all sorts of endangered animals, as well as find out about what WWF is doing to save animals all over the world.

National Geographic

www.nationalgeographic.com/animals/reptiles

Find out about different reptiles, their natural habitats and the threats they face.

GLOSSARY

adapted	changed over time to suit an environment
aquatic	living in or near water
bloodstream	the blood that flows through the body of a person or animal
camouflage	colours, shapes or patterns that help an animal to hide in its environment
energy	the power required for an activity
extinction	the process of a species dying out
grasslands	large areas of dry land covered in small bushes and trees
limbs	arms, legs and wings
mate	to produce young with an animal of the same species
organs	parts of animals that have specific, important jobs
oxygen	a gas that all living things need in order to survive
parasites	living things that survive by feeding off live animals or plants
pollution	the act of adding harmful things to the environment
predators	animals that hunt other animals for food
prey	animals that are hunted by other animals
species	a group of very similar animals that are capable of producing young together
tropical regions	warm and wet areas near the equator
unique	unlike anything else
venom	a harmful substance that comes from a bite or a sting
vertebrate	an animal with a backbone

INDEX